Picture credits:
l: Left, r: Right, t: Top, b: Bottom, c: Centre

Front Cover Images: Front Cover: Reiulf Grønnevik/Shutterstock: tl, Joel Calheiros/Shutterstock: tm, Jason Lugo/istock: tr, Kitch Bain/Shutterstock: ml, Rafal Fabrykiewicz/istock: mr, bukvarj/Shutterstock: b, vera bogaerts/Shutterstock: bl, Thomas Nord/Shutterstock: bm, Andre Nantel/Shuttestock: br, SERDAR YAGCI/istock: extreme br,

Back Cover Images : Marek Slusarczyk/istock: t, Vera Bogaerts/Shutterstock: b.

Border Images: Chee-Onn Leong/Shutterstock, coko/Shutterstock, Efremova Irina/Shutterstock, Maksym Gorpenyuk/Shutterstock, Kris Vandereycken/Shutterstock, Vadim Kozlovsky/Shutterstock

Dmitry Savinov/Shutterstock: 6, Jason Scott Duggan/Shutterstock: 7bl, Craig Hill/Shutterstock: 7r, Tan Wei Ming/Shutterstock: 8, Sergge /Dreamstime: 9t, Mikhail Olykainen /Shutterstock: 10tr, Elnur/Shutterstock: 10b, Galina Barskaya/Shutterstock: 11t, eAlisa/Shutterstock: 11b, Gavriel Jecan: 12-13t, Mark Atkins/Shutterstock: 12bl, lebanmax/Shutterstock: 13b, Oleksandr Bondar/dreamstime: 14, Elke Dennis/Shutterstock: 15t, George Burba/Shutterstock: 15b, Serghei Starus/Shutterstock: 17m, Cappi Thompson/Shutterstock: 18, Steve Simzer/Shutterstock: 19t, Sklep Spozywczy/Shutterstock: 20tl, Andreas G. Karelias/Shutterstock: 20-21m, Jeffrey Clattenburg/dreamstime: 21tl, Miodrag Gajic/dreamstime: 22, Marek Cech/dreamstime:23b, Arne Trautmann/Shutterstock: 25r, WHO/TDR/Crump: 25tf, Gumenuk Vitalij/dreamstime: 26, pxlar8/Shutterstock: 28, FloridaStock/shutterstock: 29, Johan Swanepoel/Shutterstock: 31br, NOAA: 31tl, Kativ/istock: 33b, Chad McDermott: 32bl, pending: 32t, Vadim Kozlovsky/Shutterstock: 34-35b, Luis M. Seco/Shutterstock: 35ml, Mike King/dreamstime: 35tr, Racico/bigstock: 36 , Slavoljub Pantelic/Shutterstock:37bl, Petr Nad/Shutterstock: 37t, Jostein Hauge/Shutterstock: 38, Jean-Yves Benedeyt/istock: 39m,

Published By: Robert Frederick Ltd.
4 North Parade, Bath, BA1 1LF, UK

First Published: 2008
All rights reserved. No part of this publication may be reprinted, stored in a retrieval system or transmitted, in any form or by any means, electronic, mechanical, photocopying, recording, or otherwise, without the prior permission of the copyright holder.

While every effort has been made to verify the information within as correct at the time of going to print, the publisher cannot accept responsibility for any errors or omissions that may occur.

Planet in Crisis

CONTENTS

Treasure Trove	6
Increasing Numbers	8
Space to Live	10
Food to Eat	12
Where are all the Fish?	14
Food for Us?	16
Luxuries for Man	18
Finding Fuel	20
Where's the Water?	22
Air Polution	24
Burning Earth	26
Animals in Danger	28
Ozone Hole	30
Disappearing Resources	32
Rubbish Heap	34
Red Alert	36
Dangerous Rain	38
Facts at a Glance	40
Young Activist	42
Glossary	44
Index	45

Treasure Trove

Rainforests are treasure troves of natural resources

Natural resources are incredibly valuable. They include air, water, sunlight, land, plants and animals and surround all of us every day.

Resources are Important to us

Life on earth depends on natural resources. So, a resource is something that is useful to us. The more natural resources a country has, the richer it is likely to be. Resources can be classified as renewable and non-renewable.

ECO fact

Renewable resources have to be given time to renew themselves. Rainforests are being cut down so fast, experts fear they will disappear. Using resources carefully is called sustainable use.

PLANET in crisis

Renewable Resources

Anything that can be made again is a renewable resource. Most renewable resources are living things such as animals, insects, trees and plants. But not all are living things. Sunlight, wind and tides are called 'flow' renewable resources, because they are continuous. Although water is a renewable resource only 3% of the total water on earth is usable. The rest is either frozen or too salty to use.

Non-Renewable Resources

Anything that takes a long time to be made again is a non-renewable natural resource. Coal and oil are non-renewable resources. That is because it takes millions of years for coal and oil to form. Other non-renewable natural resources include: natural gas; minerals such as diamonds; metals like iron ore, copper, gold and silver. The amount of a resource that is available, the time it takes to be made, and its use to us, decides the value or the price of the natural resource.

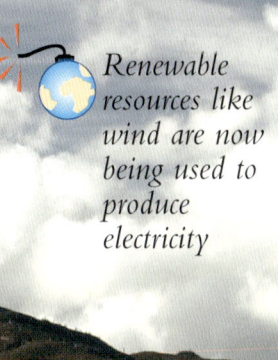
Renewable resources like wind are now being used to produce electricity

Coal is one of the most commonly used non-renewable natural resources

Increasing Numbers

A collection of people living in a certain place is known as population. The total number of people on earth is called world population.

Growing, Growing, Groan!

Counting the population of a place is called a census. The earliest known census was in Babylon in 3800 BC. The oldest census we can still find records for was taken in 2 AD in China during the Han dynasty. In 1 AD, there were an estimated 200,000 people in the world. By 1804, it was 1 billion. By 1961, it was 3 billion. It took just 13 years to increase that to 4 billion. In 2007, there were over 6.6 billion people on earth. It is projected that by 2011 there will be seven billion people living on this planet!

China has the largest population in the world - over 1.3 billion people!

Increasing population has led to more crowded towns and cities

PLANET in crisis

The Biggest Growth

The last 100 years have seen a rapid increase in population. Medicines and healthcare have improved and lengthened lifespan. Better agriculture means many people have enough to eat. Communications and travel have also improved.

Continent Count

Asia is home to around 3.8 billion people. Africa has about 840 million people. The Americas have around 885 million. Europe comes next with 710 million people and Australia has 21 million. China is the most populated country with 1.32 billion people. India has 1.12 billion and the United States of America comes third with 300 million people.

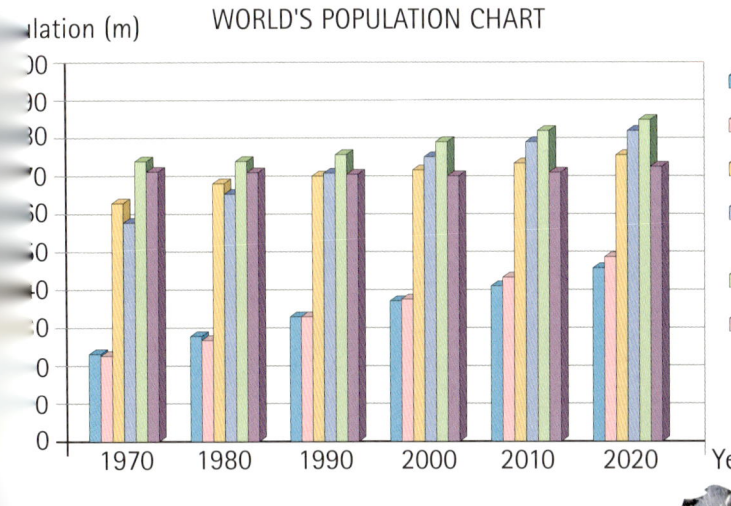

WORLD'S POPULATION CHART
- Africa
- Asia
- Europe
- Latin America & the Caribbean
- North America
- Oceania

ECO fact

The world's population has never been younger. In 2007, about 27 per cent of the world's population was below 15 years old.

Space to Live

Every day, more than 200,000 babies join this world. In just the last two centuries the world's population has grown more than sixfold! All these people need space to live.

A Roof Over Every Head

Populations have grown but the amount of land has not. So, large sections of land that was covered with forests for centuries is now being cleared for new homes, townships and cities. In the past 200 years, the area under dense rainforests has fallen from 1,500 million hectares to 750 million hectares. The tropical region, or the land extending from the Equator to the Tropic of Cancer in the northern hemisphere, and to the Tropic of Capricorn in the southern hemisphere, has very thick forests and a huge variety of wildlife. These rainforests have been around for millions of years. About a hundred years ago, they occupied around 14% of the land surface. Today, they cover only 6%. If they continue to be cut at this rate, rainforests could be gone in less than 40 years, taking with them half the world's trees and wildlife!

Vast areas of forest are cleared every day to make space for farming and housing and to provide raw materials

ECO fact

Total forest cover has fallen by half in the last 50 years. In 1990, forests covered 4,077 million hectares. In 2005, that fell to 3,952 million hectares, a fall of about 8 million hectares a year.

PLANET in crisis

Wood For Every Chair

Trees are cut for a number of reasons: land is cleared to mine for minerals; wood is required for making homes and furniture; wood is also used as fuel and to make paper; forests are cleared to set up hydroelectric projects to meet growing electricity demands; roads are cut through forests for new human settlements. Some experts fear that in the last 50 years, some 600,000 plant and animal species have gone forever. The world has not lost so many plants and animals since the dinosaurs became extinct!

Trees are cut for wood to make furniture and to keep us warm

Fill 'Em Up

As populations swell, lakes and ponds in some areas are being filled-in to create more land. At the same time, rising sea levels threaten the world's coastlines. The loss of forests and the increasing use of fossil fuels have led to the world warming by about 0.5 degrees Celsius (32.9 degrees Fahrenheit) in the last 40 years. This is melting glaciers and releasing more water into rivers and seas. With the water level rising, coastal lands are being swallowed up, with the potential to displace millions of people!

New land is created not only by filling in rivers and lakes, but also by artificially extending the coast

Food to Eat

As the population grows, we need more food to feed the millions, requiring more farmland and water for irrigation.

Give Me More!

Most of our food comes from the land. Grain needs land to grow on and animals need land to graze on. From the time early hunter-gatherers settled down and turned to agriculture, forest cover has been reducing. Most of this loss has been in the past two centuries as populations grew and we cleared forests for farmland. 40 per cent of the land on earth has been brought under agriculture and grazing cattle by human beings.

Over-grazing has left many places in Africa barren and vulnerable to drought

Not Enough Land

Land for crops is reducing for several reasons. Trees help to break the wind. When you cut trees down, the topsoil is swept away. This happened at Karamay Agricultural Development Region in Xinjiang, China. In some places, the fertile topsoil has been washed away by rain and floods. The overuse of chemical fertilizers can also make soil infertile. Huge hydroelectric projects are taking away acres of farmland. Moreover, many farmers are not aware of the dangers of pumping too much water onto land, making it infertile.

Trees are being cut to make way for farm land

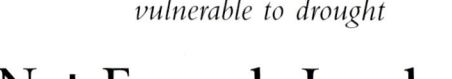

PLANET in crisis

ECO fact

One out of every three apples grown in the UK lands in the rubbish bin. The amount of food wasted in the country has been rising by 15 per cent every 10 years.

Let's Look Further

With the growing need for food we continue to look for more and more agricultural land. Forests are cleared to provide people with more land to grow crops on. About sixty per cent of the trees cut are to make way for agricultural fields. Thousands of different plant and animal species thrive in forests, enriching ecological diversity. Every time a forest is cleared it takes away the natural habitats of these plants and animals. Instead of concentrating on making more land available for agriculture, it is perhaps more important to improve the quality of land that is available to us. That way we will not need more land.

Over-ploughing can strip soil of its fertility and can cause the loss of valuable topsoil

Where are all the Fish?

Overfishing threatens about a third of the world's species of fish, with numbers reduced to below 10 per cent of previously recorded populations.

Modern trawlers use large nets to comb the bottom of the sea, damaging all in their path

Something Fishy

In 1950 about 18m tonnes of fish was landed. By 1969 this had increased to 56m tonnes. However, the population of fish did not grow proportionately. The coastal anchovy fisheries of Peru, for example, produced 10.2m metric tonnes in 1971. The next year, the stocks were down to less than 1m metric tonnes. In 1992, overfishing led Canada to stop fishing on the Grand Banks.

Growing Unlike A Whale

The hunting of whales is banned by many countries. Dspite this, today five out of thirteen great whale species, including the massive blue whale, are endangered due to commercial whaling. During the 19th and 20th centuries whales were widely hunted for their meat and oil. Even today whale oil is in demand, prompting some countries to continue to whale.

PLANET in crisis

In the Soup

The next time you are tempted to order a bowl of shark fin soup, remind yourself that many fins are cut from living sharks, who are then thrown back into the sea to die. The IUCN red list says 39 species of sharks and rays are threatened. In just the last 50 years, the numbers of some shark species have fallen by 50 per cent. The basking shark, the whale shark and the great white shark are threatened species.

ECO fact

It is thought that as much as 70 per cent of fish sold as the highly prized red snapper is in fact another species! This is a phenomenon known as 'species substitution'.

Whale bones are highly prized in some remote Arctic regions

Shark fin soup is a delicacy in countries like China

Food For Us?

In 1998, nearly 280 biologists told the American Museum of Natural History that several species of animals will be wiped out because of human activity.

Mammoths were hunted into extinction by early man

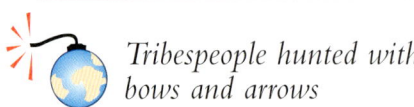

Tribespeople hunted with bows and arrows

Killing Them Off

Since 1500 BC, about 784 species have become extinct. Humans are the biggest threat to other forms of life. Our activities kill other species in several ways: factories release poisonous gases that pollute the atmosphere and untreated waste matter that pollutes lakes, rivers and seas, killing creatures that live there; irresponsible hunting has led to many species becoming extinct; every time a forest is cleared, we lose mammals, birds and insects.

PLANET in crisis

Almost Gone

The great mammoths may have been threatened by disease or by a change in the climate. But many biologists believe they were hunted by the Clovis, a tribe of nomadic hunters. About 500 years ago, North America had 30 million buffalo and bison. Around 10 million of them were killed on the Great Plains in just 10 years. By the late 19th century, their numbers were in serious decline. They were killed for meat and leather, and sometimes also for sport. Today, the European bison is still endangered. If they are not protected we may lose them forever.

ECO fact

Human beings are the only animals that hunt for pleasure. All other animals kill for food or to defend themselves. Humans are also the only species that use weapons to kill.

Rarer meats are often considered a delicacy and can fetch higher prices as a result

Deserted

Life is difficult in the desert. Hunting and loss of habitat makes this life even more difficult! The goitered gazelle, for example, was the most common of all gazelle species. Today, in the deserts of Mongolia, where it once roamed, very few remain. The dama gazelle, once found in 12 countries, may soon become extinct with only 300 left in the world. The scimitar-horned oryx is already extinct.

Luxuries for Man

For centuries, people have hunted for fun. Deer antlers, tiger skins, tiger claws and teeth, bison horns and elephant tusks have been hung as trophies.

Hunting ranches in the US allow people to hunt exotic animals such as the Indian blackbuck and other rare African antelope

Is This Sport?

In the name of sport, people have been inflicting injuries and death on animals for hundreds of years. Bullfighting often leaves the bull bleeding to death. Racing greyhounds is a billion-pound industry, but old or injured greyhounds are often neglected. Such activity has led to the formation of many action groups that aim to change government legislation. For example, The League Against Cruel Sports, set up in 1924, tries to stop cruelty to animals for sport.

Cold Comfort

Shahtoosh is a Persian word that means 'pleasure of the king'. It was woven from the soft hair of the Chiru antelope found in Kashmir, India. A pure shahtoosh shawl is so soft, it can be passed through a ring. This made the shahtoosh very expensive and popular. Originally, the shahtoosh was made from fur that the Chiru shed once a year. But this soon changed. With demand rising, the antelope was hunted nearly to extinction. Today, it is an endangered animal and the shahtoosh has been banned.

Tooth And Nail

Tigers are some of the most endangered animals in the world. Despite this, the mighty tiger is still hunted in some places. It is sometimes hunted for its bones, which are made into tablets and wine by doctors of traditional Chinese medicine to cure joint pain. The bones are also boiled and made into a paste that is believed to make you as strong as a tiger. Almost every part of a tiger's body is used by people. That makes the majestic tiger a popular target for hunting.

Elephants and rhinos have been hunted extensively for their tusks, which are used to make expensive trinkets

Tigers were extensively hunted for sport as well as for their skin, teeth and claws

ECO fact

Snake charmers have fooled people in India and Pakistan for hundreds of years: snakes do not dance to music because they are deaf! Rather, they sway to the movement of the snake charmer.

Finding Fuel

We need energy for all kinds of activities, from driving, to cooking and flying an aeroplane. Anything that can be used to produce energy is known as a fuel. Wood, coal and different oils have been used as fuel for thousands of years.

Touch Wood

Wood is an abundant natural energy source. It is used for cooking and heating. Wood is very versatile as logs, charcoal or sawdust. The demand for wood is enormous and vast areas of forest are cleared every day to meet demand. Burning wood releases smoke, which contains carbon dioxide and other chemicals that pollute the air.

In many countries wood is still used to warm homes during winter

Tarred By Coal

Coal is formed from the remains of plants. That is why it is called a fossil fuel. People have used coal for thousands of years. Coal fuelled the Industrial Revolution when many machines, including trains, required coal for running. It is also used to produce electricity. Forests are often cleared to make way for coal mines. Coal releases methane gas and produces harmful greenhouse gases like carbon dioxide, sulphur and nitrogen oxide. These cause global warming and acid rain.

Coal-fired power plants are still very popular as they are one of the cheapest ways to generate electricity

PLANET in crisis

Not Much Cleaner

Environmentalists are worried that burning fossil fuels releases greenhouse gases and leads to global warming. Over time, other forms of fuel have been developed from plants. Scientists have developed biofuels, or agro fuels, such as bioethanol from maize and biodiesel from rapeseed. However, it has been proved recently that these biofuels can release nitrous oxide and lead to as much greenhouse gases as other fossil fuels. So, these forms of fuel are not really safer than fossil fuels. Moreover, growing plants for fuel also means more forests have to be cut to make way for crops.

Car manufacturers are now making cars that can run on hydrogen instead of fossil fuels

ECO fact

The world went through a huge energy crisis around 1973. People gave energy more thought than ever before. There was even a magazine on energy named Wood Burning Quarterly!

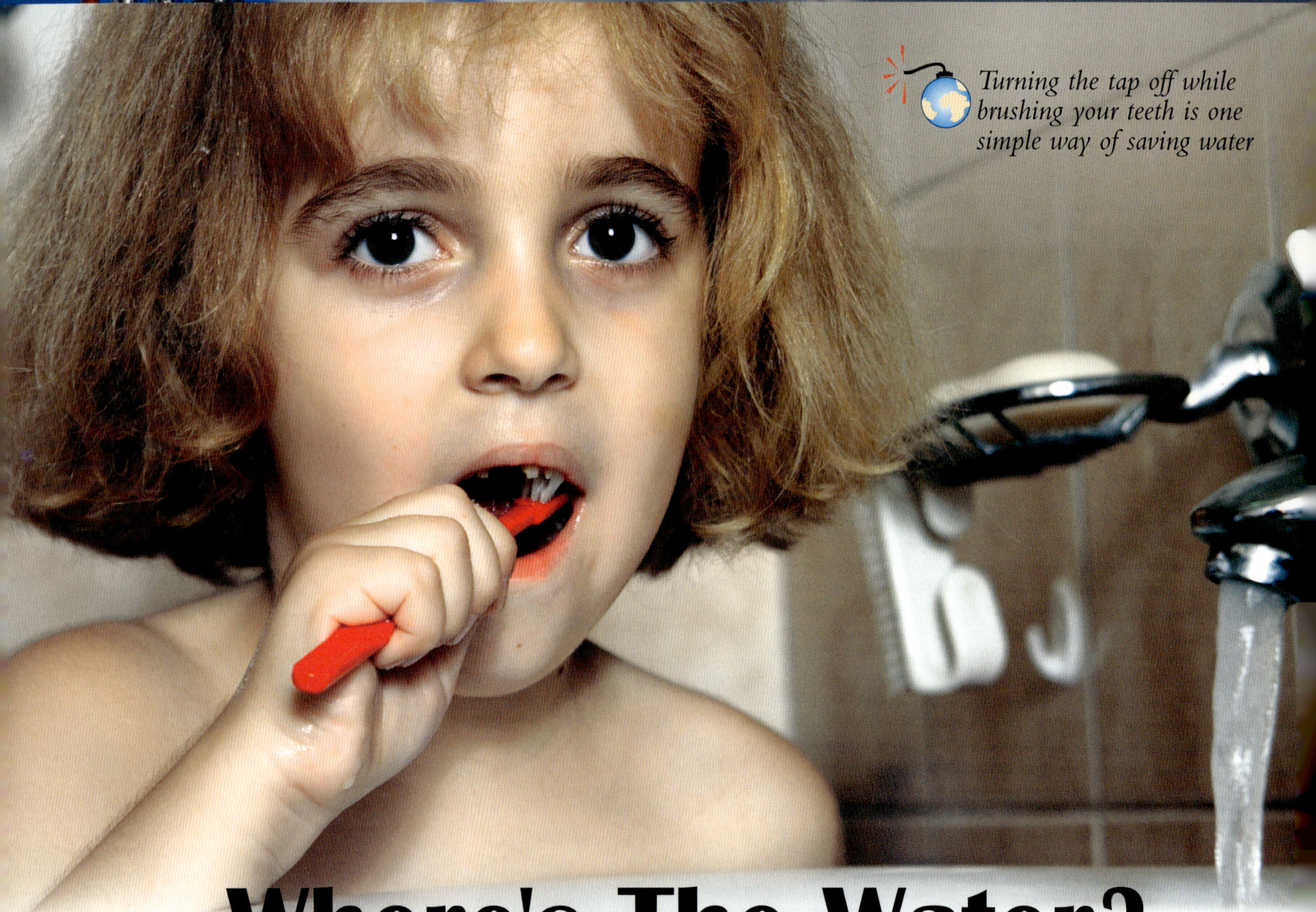

Turning the tap off while brushing your teeth is one simple way of saving water

Where's The Water?

Three quarters of the world's surface is covered by water. Yet still there is not enough water for all our needs!

Water, Water Everywhere

We use water for domestic purposes, such as to drink and wash with, and also for industrial purposes such as generating hydroelectric energy. Water is used in religious ceremonies like baptisms and in festivals like the Thingyan water festival in Burma (Myanmar). Water is a natural resource which needs to be conserved and used sensibly.

ECO fact

In 2000, over two million people died because the rains failed and caused drought or because of diseases caused by dirty water.

PLANET in crisis

Even Under The Surface

The level below the ground where water is found is called the water table. The water table is fed by the rains. Water is pumped up for homes, farms and factories. But we are pumping up more water than comes down with the rains. In 2000, the world fell short of 35 million tonnes of grain due to drought. In 2001, it was 31 million tonnes.

WATER TABLE

Water Riots

Water is growing so scarce that people have begun fighting over it. In some places taps are kept under lock and key. In 2000, three farmers died in a protest over giving water to the town of Jamnagar in India. In September 2007, a judge noted that almost half the murder cases from Punjab, the most prosperous farming state in India, were over water!

The increasing demand for water has led to a gross reduction in ground water in some places. This, combined with lack of rains, might soon lead to a critical lack of ground water in some places

Lack of rain in many places in Asia, Africa and Australia have led to long months of drought

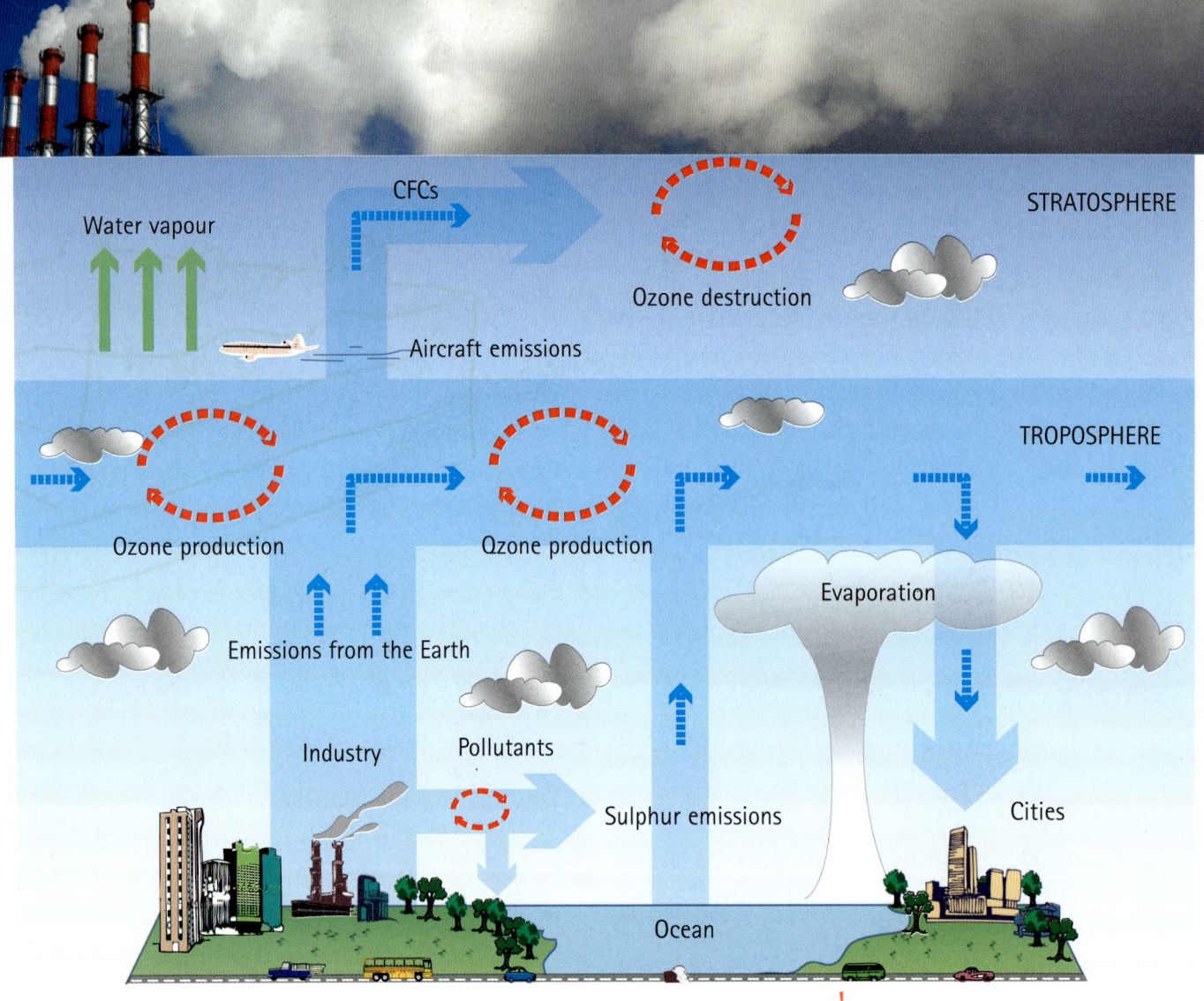

The causes of global warming

Air Pollution

Air pollution is a serious concern both in the short-term and for future generations.

Heat Can Kill

Over the last 100 years, the earth has been heating up. This is called global warming. Temperatures are predicted to rise by 1.1-6.4 degrees Centigrade (2.0-11.5 degrees Fahrenheit) by the end of this century. While volcanic eruptions can cause some of it, most of it is because of industry and other activities by humans, releasing more greenhouse gases into the atmosphere. Global warming has caused changes in the climate and the water levels in the world. It has also affected plant and animal life.

ECO fact

In December 1984, a leak from the Union Carbide factory in Bhopal, India, left more than 2,000 people dead in hours. 6,000 more died from problems caused by the gas leak.

PLANET in crisis

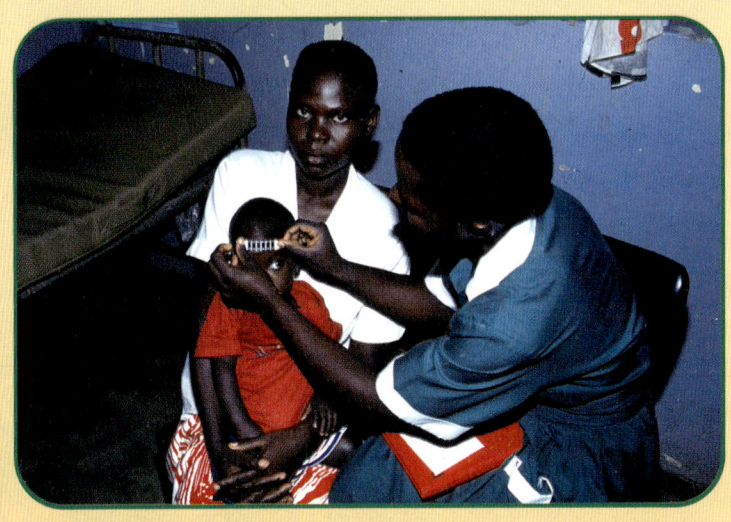

 *Air pollution affects children the most, causing respiratory illnesses and other problems*

Call the Doctor!

The 1990s was the hottest decade for a thousand years. Global warming may cause diseases to spread, since some germs survive better in warmer temperatures. Dangerous illnesses like yellow fever, malaria, cholera, typhoid, chikungunya, dengue are already on the rise. Schistosomiasis, lymphatic filariasis, leishmaniasis, American trypanosomiasis, or Chaga's disease, and river blindness, or onchoceriasis, may also increase.

Poison In The Air

Scientists have known about air pollution for many years. Now, it can be seen from space. At the start of this century, NASA's *Terra* spacecraft tracked air pollution around the world. The World Health Organisation estimates that 2.4 million deaths a year can be attributed to air pollution, through the development of breathing problems like bronchitis and asthma, along with heart and other lung diseases.

 *Excessive smoke from factories and vehicles causes smog*

Burning Earth

As temperatures rise, so many parts of the earth are exposed to more extreme heat, with the many risks that that brings.

Weather Report

With summers getting hotter and longer, more people are falling ill with heat-related diseases and incidences of death from heat stroke around the world are on the rise. In 2003, about 35,000 people died in heat waves that hit Europe. With the world getting warmer, more violent storms are being recorded than ever before. Hurricanes Katrina and Rita caused massive damage. Crops that prefer cold weather like wheat, mustard, chickpea, lentil and some types of potato have less time to grow. The number of forest fires has been on the rise too. These can spread over massive areas and destroy everything in their path.

Melting Ice

The earth has about 160,000 glaciers. Almost all of them have been slowly melting away for the last century. While some of this is natural, most of it is because of human activity. They have melted the most since the mid-1990s. If glaciers continue to melt at this rate, most of them may melt away in another 50 years. Thousands of glaciers in the Himalayas are melting. The extra water is filling up mountain lakes in Nepal and Bhutan. If the water does not evaporate fast enough, the lakes will flood their banks. When this water flows down, sea levels will rise, threatening coastal regions.

Incidents of wildfires are on the increase in many countries, including the US and Australia

PLANET in crisis

Goodbye To Many Things

As the world gets warmer, things we have taken for granted may be in danger. If France gets any warmer, for example, it may affect the growth of grapes and the making of wine, which will have to shift to cooler places. Pests like the pine bark beetle thrive in warm weather and attack forests of the Christmas tree pine in British Columbia. Antarctica, the white continent, has reported a new colour in winter: green, with tufts of grass showing in places they haven't been see previously.

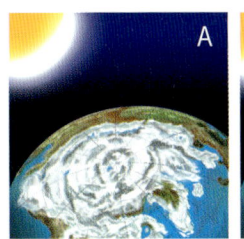  

 *Some scientists believe that the permanent ice layer covering the Arctic is reducing by 9 per cent every 10 years*

 *Global warming has led to the melting of more than 13,000 sq km (5,019 sq miles) of sea ice in the Antarctic over the last 50 years*

ECO fact

Since 1987, there have been increasing numbers of forest fires in the USA, burning more land than ever before. Global warming causes longer dry spells that encourage these fires.

Animals In Danger

Human activity over the last four hundred years has had a huge impact on the earth. At least 784 animal species have been lost forever. The IUCN believes that 16,119 animal and plant species are endangered.

Polar Tragedy

As ice in Polar regions melts, animals such as polar bears begin to suffer as their habitat suffers. Although they are strong swimmers, they are land animals. With less land to rest on, scientists fear polar bears will drown from the exhaustion of having to swim greater distances between ice floes. Global warming is threatening the habitat of penguins as well. In recent years, the number of pairs of breeding emperor penguins have fallen dramatically in the western Antarctic Peninsula.

The rise in sea temperature is leading to what is called coral bleaching, wherein coral reefs lose their magnificent colour

ECO fact

Migrating Siberian cranes that previously flew in winter to India are rarely seen there today as most of them have been hunted during their flight over Central Asia.

PLANET in crisis

The increase in temperature is slowly leading to the depletion of wetlands - the habitat of Siberian cranes - causing these birds to migrate longer distances for survival

Coral Grief

Coral reefs have been around for over 200 million years. Fish, corals, crabs and lobsters, jellyfish and sponges all find a home in and around coral reefs. With oxygen levels in the water falling, coral reefs are dying and so is the life they support. Untreated waste water from sewage, industries, pollution from ships and pesticides cause diseases in the coral reefs. Rising sea temperatures cause coral bleaching, where the coral turns white. Since 1979, more than 60 coral reefs have experienced this phenomena. If water pollution continues at the same rate, coral reefs could soon be under great threat!

Flying Into Trouble

Some of the world's birds are under great threat as a result of human activity. Those that prey on insects are dying from the pesticides sprayed on crops. These include bobwhites and sparrows. Vultures, which eat dead animals, are also perishing because the animals they feed on are dying of poisoning from chemicals. Thousands of birds die every year on power lines or after hitting aircrafts, offshore oil rigs and wind turbines.

Ozone Hole

The ozone is an invisible layer of the atmosphere above the earth. It protects the earth from the harmful ultraviolet (UV) rays of the sun.

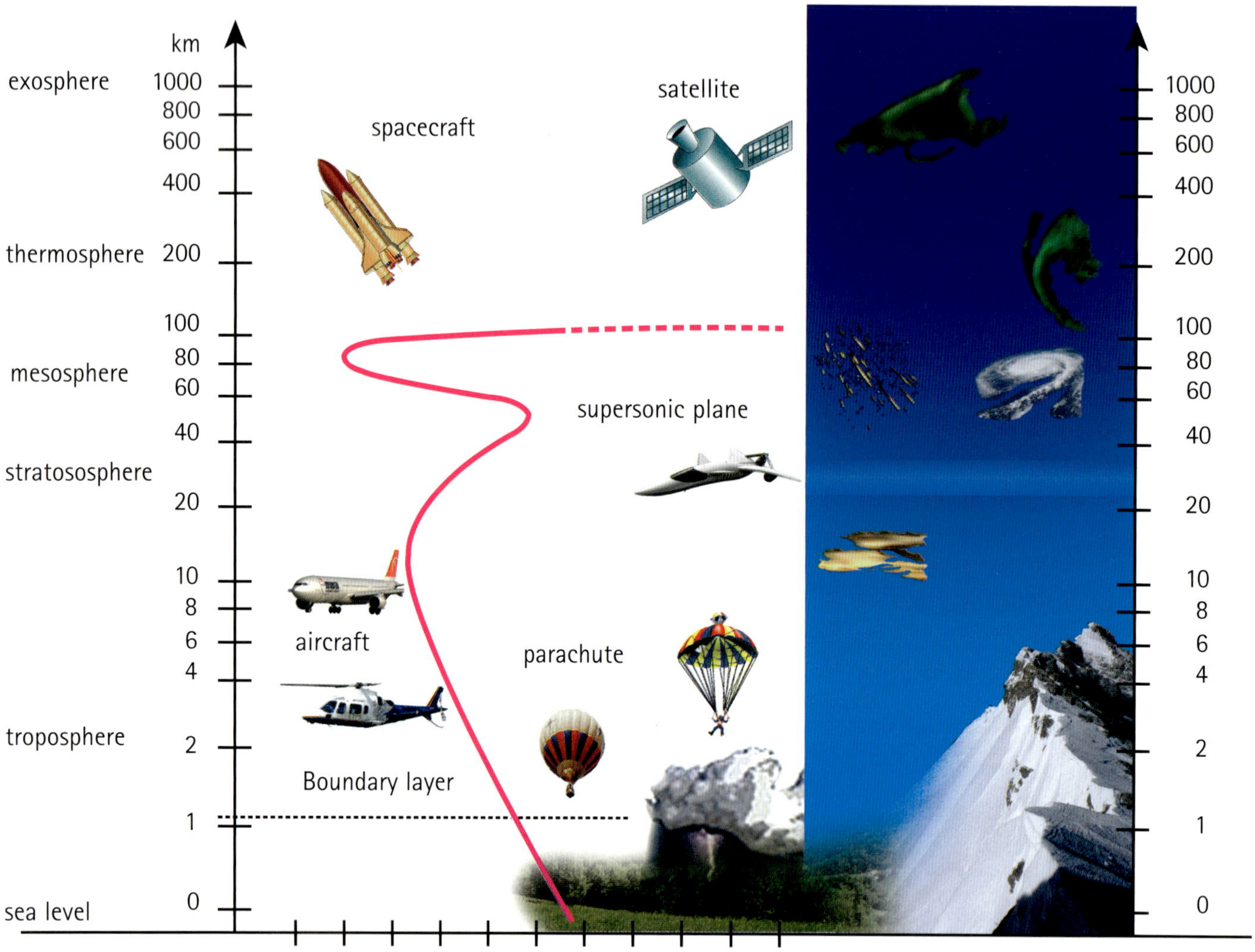

More About The Blanket

In 1913, French scientists Charles Fabry and Henri Buisson discovered the ozone layer. It stretches from 15-35 km (9-21 miles) above the surface of the earth. The ozone layer is of uneven thickness; less over the equator and more at the poles. Its density is high in spring, low in autumn and increases in winter.

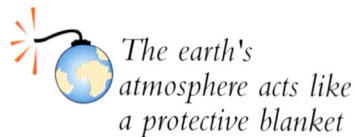

The earth's atmosphere acts like a protective blanket

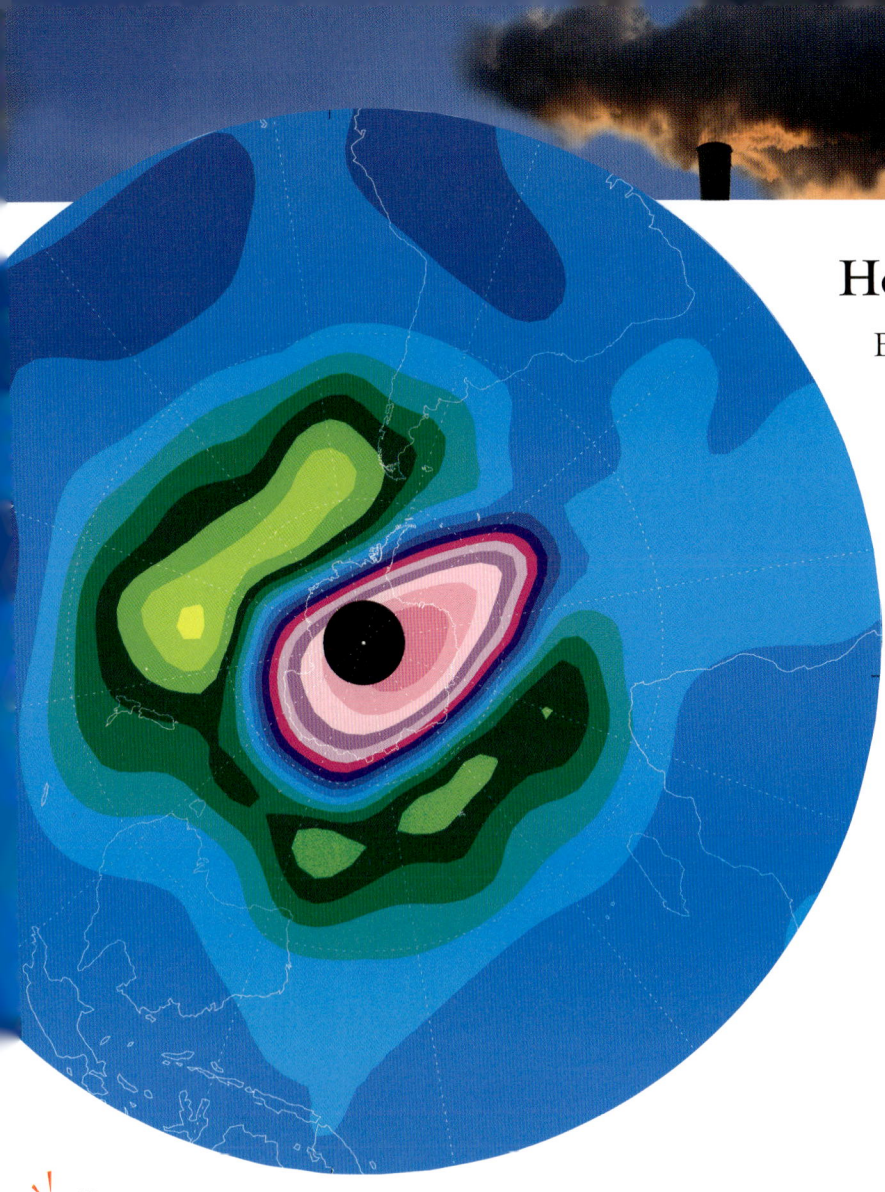

Holes In The Blanket

By the 1980s, it was well publicised that the ozone layer was decreasing. As a result certain health problems have increased, including incidences of skin cancer and cataracts.

ECO fact

British weatherman, G. M. B. Dobson, first measured the ozone layer with a spectrophotometer. The Dobson unit, used for ozone measurements, is named after him.

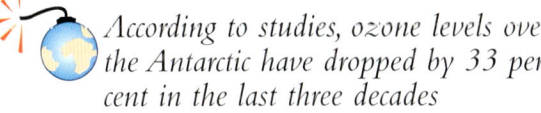
According to studies, ozone levels over the Antarctic have dropped by 33 per cent in the last three decades

Is This Also Human Made?

The thinning or depletion of the ozone layer is attributed to several factors. One of the biggest culprits is bromofluorocarbons (BFCs) and chlorofluorocarbons (CFCs), gases used in industry, in refrigerators, and to make sprays, foam and soap. CFCs rise through the atmosphere to the stratosphere, where they release chlorine. The chlorine atoms first join with ozone molecules and then break them apart. Other culprits include chemicals like methyl bromide, found in pesticides, and halons in fire extinguishers.

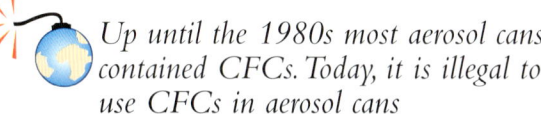
Up until the 1980s most aerosol cans contained CFCs. Today, it is illegal to use CFCs in aerosol cans

Disappearing Resources

Earth's natural resources are now gradually depleting due to human activities like deforestation.

There are hardly 7,000 tigers left in the world today

Slipping On An Oil Slick

In 1956, M. King Hubbert drew up the Hubbert peak theory, or the peak oil theory. He believed that oil reserves were limited and that oil was being drawn from the earth faster than it was regenerating. It's now widely accepted that oil wells will run dry.

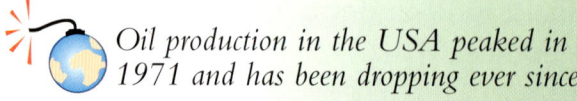
Oil production in the USA peaked in 1971 and has been dropping ever since

PLANET in crisis

On Their Way Out

Animals, plants, birds and insects can become extinct because of natural reasons. But the man-made causes are far more serious. Present extinction rates are at least 100 times greater than what the natural speed of extinction should be. 7,266 animal species and 8,323 plant and lichen species face extinction today. Species that have recently become extinct include the Hawaiian crow. Most of these threatened species are found in the Asian and African continents.

Panda Pandemonium

The giant panda is the symbol of the World Wide Fund for Nature (WWF), formed in 1961. The panda's future is in danger. Each panda needs to eat 12-38 kg (26.5-83.8 lbs) of bamboo a day. But with human activity eating into forests, the panda's bamboo is under threat in China, where the panda is found. Poachers continue to kill them. The Chinese government had set up over 50 panda reserves by 2005. But only about 980 pandas are in these reserves.

There are only about 3,000 pandas left in the world

ECO fact

Coal is depleting fast. West Yorkshire was a busy mining area for over a century. But the mines began to run out of coal. In 2002, the Prince of Wales was the last mine to close.

Rubbish Heap

Rubbish, and what to do with it, is one of the biggest challenges facing our world today. As consumers, almost everything we buy produces waste.

First Tip

Rubbish disposal has long been a problem. Archaeologists believe they have found the earliest rubbish tip, in Athens, dating from around 400 BC. By 200 BC, rubbish was becoming a real problem. So, the Romans employed the first bin men to collect rubbish! In the modern world, the English Parliament banned the dumping of waste in public places in 1388. The amount of rubbish is growing everyday and its impact upon the earth is set only to increase, unless we can find innovative ways of reducing the amount of rubbish we produce.

ECO fact

The first Earth Day was celebrated on 22 April, 1970, to make people aware of the dangers of rubbish and pollution.

Rubbish is most commonly buried in landfills

PLANET in crisis

How Rubbish Changes

The nature of rubbish has changed over the years. 1868 saw the first celluloid, or synthetic, plastic. Soon, plastic was being utilized, where wood, metal and bones were used previously. Other inventions that changed rubbish include cellophane (used in plastic packaging), aluminium foil, throwaway items like ballpoint pens and lighters, polyethylene-lined paper, styrofoam cups and disposable razors. By 1963, drinks cans had made their way on to shop shelves.

Recyclable waste ends up in a recycling centre where it is processed into raw materials to be used again

The Three Rs

The three Rs aim to reduce rubbish. Remember: reduce, reuse and recycle. If each of us reduces the amount of stuff we throw out, it makes a huge difference. There are many things we can reuse, such as plastic bags. More rubbish than you might think can be recycled.

Rubbish should be divided into biodegradable, recyclable and non-recyclable waste

Red Alert

Waste can be harmful to our health. Toxic or dangerous waste is mainly made up of chemicals that can poison living things, including trees, insects and animals.

From All Over

Toxic waste has been increasing since the Industrial Revolution. Most toxic waste comes from factories, hospitals and agriculture. These sources can release chemicals into water, land and the air. Toxic wastes include mercury, lead, asbestos and acid from batteries. They can cause birth defects, illnesses like cancer and may kill many people and animals.

Over the last couple of decades diseases like cancer and respiratory diseases have been on the rise

ECO fact

Nuclear waste includes plutonium, uranium and other radioactive elements. Most of them emit large amounts of radiation. They can stay active for as long as 100,000 years.

PLANET in crisis

Toxic Trade

Believe it or not, toxic waste is actually traded! Industries in developed countries sell toxic waste to countries that often have less stringent regulations about how it is processed. For years, shiploads of toxic waste have been sent to Papua New Guinea, the Philippines, India and Russia to be recycled.

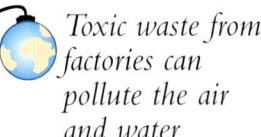
Toxic waste from factories can pollute the air and water

Can The Waste Be Treated?

Toxic waste can be treated. However, it is expensive and a matter of international debate. In 1989, about 50 countries signed The Basel Convention on the Control of Transboundary Movement of Hazardous Wastes and their Disposal, a treaty to regulate dumping toxic waste. Toxic waste can also be produced by hospitals that treat diseases like cancer with radiation therapy. This kind of waste needs to be isolated and disposed of carefully. Nuclear waste is the result of nuclear fission. A large amount of nuclear waste stored under Lake Karachay in Russia has been dispersed by storms as the lake has dried up over the years. Indeed, the lake is said to be the most polluted place on the planet!

Most countries have strict laws about disposal of toxic waste

Dangerous Rain

Acid rain is rainfall that has a pH level of less than 5.6. An acid has a sour taste, like vinegar or limejuice. It can fall to earth as rain, hail, snow or sleet.

Acid rain seeps into trees through the roots, preventing them from taking in carbon dioxide for photosynthesis, eventually killing them

Recent Downpour

The first acid rain was noticed in Manchester in 1852. Since the Industrial Revolution, more and more sulphur dioxide and nitrogen oxide has been released into the atmosphere. Factories, vehicles and electricity generators are the principal culprits. Acid rain has been increasing over the last ten years and threatens lakes and rivers across the world. The polluting vapours can travel hundreds of kilometres. Chemicals like sulphur dioxide (SO_2) are produced by industries and from burning fossil fuels. Even volcanoes can release acid gases. Acid rain has been around for thousands of years, but it has increased to dangerous amounts recently.

PLANET in crisis

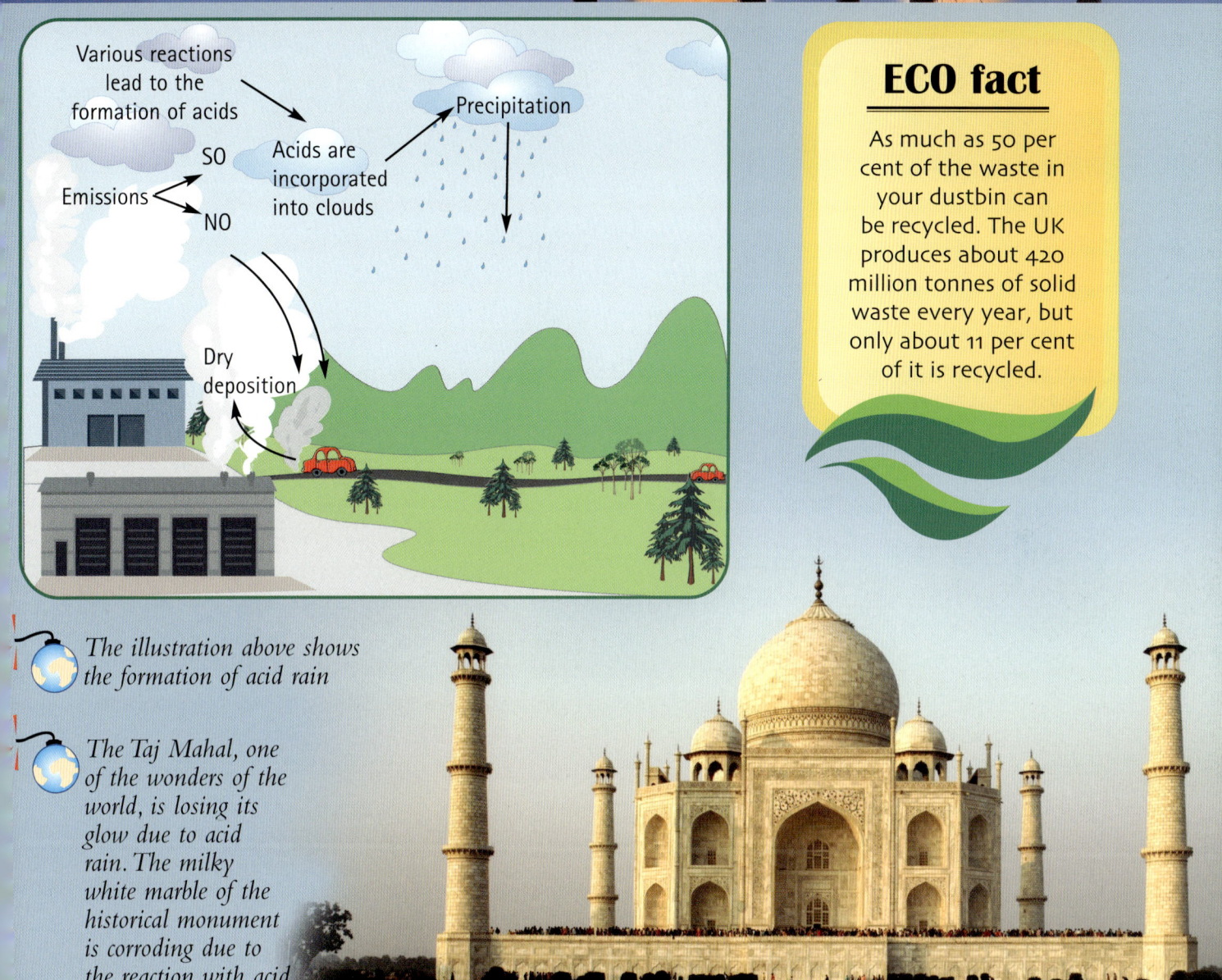

🌍 The illustration above shows the formation of acid rain

🌍 The Taj Mahal, one of the wonders of the world, is losing its glow due to acid rain. The milky white marble of the historical monument is corroding due to the reaction with acid

ECO fact

As much as 50 per cent of the waste in your dustbin can be recycled. The UK produces about 420 million tonnes of solid waste every year, but only about 11 per cent of it is recycled.

What It Does

Acid is corrosive. Acid rain harms anything it falls on, from buildings and statues to trees, water bodies and animals. Leaves burn and drop off and trees can get stunted. Even though some animals, such as frogs, can live in water that is more acidic, acid rain is dangerous to life. Acidic water does not allow fish roe to hatch and so threatens fish populations.

Stop That Rain!

Burning less coal will reduce the release of acids into the atmosphere. Newly built cars emit less of the poisonous nitrogen oxide. Factories that use coal can install cleaning devices like gas desulphurisation equipment to reduce the harmful sulphur gases. Our commitment to environmentally friendly choices is a good way forward in reducing acid rain.

Facts at a Glance

- Coal used worldwide: 6.2 billion tons a year
- Coal used to produce electricity: 4.65 billion tons a year
- Total petroleum deposits: 1.2 trillion barrels
- Petroleum use worldwide: 84 million barrels per day

- At least 200 cities have a population of more than a million people
- Most densely populated country: Monaco - 23,660 people per sq/km
- Least densely populated country: Greenland - 0.026 people per sq/km
- North America has 3.7 million farmers, Europe has 20.1 million and East Asia has 517.8 million people working in agriculture

PLANET in crisis

- Asia produces more than 40 per cent of the total food around the world. Oceania produces just 2.1 per cent
- Total tiger population today: 5,000 to 7,400
  Tiger population in India 100 years ago: 50,000 to 80,000

- The Amazon rainforests soak up 90-140 billion tons of carbon each year

- Metal was recycled for the first time in the USA when a statue of King George III was melted down in New York City in 1776 to be made into bullets

Young Activist

Perhaps the largest amount of recyclable material thrown away is paper. Envelopes, letters, magazines and newspapers are often just thrown in the bin. But all of this paper can easily be used again! By following the three Rs – reduce, reuse and recycle – we can make our paper go further and save trees from being cut down.

⊘ Reduce:
- Write on both sides of your notebook so that no paper is wasted
- Ask your parents whether they can receive their bills online, rather than through the post

⊘ Reuse:
- Do not throw away cards and calendars. Use the back of cards to make grocery lists
- The reverse of calendars makes great paper for paintings and collages

⊘ Recycle:
- Most houses will have a paper recycling collection service. Make sure your parents are using it. Otherwise, a lot of supermarkets have paper recycling collection points

PLANET in crisis

Make Your Own Paper

✓ **Get together:**
- old newspaper and egg cartons
- water
- wide-mouthed container
- bucket
- net screens
- flower petals from old bouquets and pencil shavings

✓ **Get going:**
- Tear up the newspaper and egg cartons as small as you can
- Soak the paper in warm water for a few days. If you want to speed it up, ask an adult to help boil the mush
- Blend it in a food processor
- Stir in flower petals and pencil shavings
- Pour the mush over the screen. Try to keep the layer of paper thin. Let it dry
- You could add some weight like books on top of the paper pulp to make your paper firmer
- Peel it off when dry. Your very own handmade paper is ready! Make it into cards or wrap gifts for friends in it!

Glossary

Anchovy: A small marine fish. Found in abundance in the Mediterranean Sea

Archaeologist: A person who studies historic or prehistoric peoples and their cultures by collecting information about their artifacts, inscriptions, architecture, and other similar remains

Biologist: A person who studies living organisms, their structure, growth, evolution and distribution

Census: An official count of the population of a place, with details of the age, sex and occupation of those who live there

Depletion: A drastic decrease in the supply of something

Displace: To force something or someone from a place or country

Disposable: designed for or capable of being thrown away after being used

Extinct: no longer in existence; that has ended or died out

Habitat: The natural environment of an animal or plant that is suitable for its life and growth

Halon: A chemical compound commonly used in fire extinguishers

Hazardous: Highly risky, or toxic

Irradiated: To be exposed to harmful radiation

Nomadic: A member of a group of people who move from place to place in search of food and water

Pesticide: A chemical substance that destroys pests that destroy crops

Poacher: A person who hunts animals illegally

Styrofoam: a light, resilient, polystyrene plastic

Trawler: A fishing boat that uses a trawl or dragnet to catch fish

Vector: An insect or any organism that acts as a carrier of disease-causing germs. For example a mosquito acts as a carrier of the organism that causes malaria

PLANET in crisis

Index

A
acid rain 20, 38, 39
Africa 9, 12, 16, 23
Amazon 41
American Museum
 of Natural History 16
Asia 9, 23, 28, 41
Australia 9, 23, 26

B
Babylon 8
basking shark 15
biofuels 21
bromofluorocarbons 31
bronchitis 25
Buisson, Henri 30
Burma (Myanmar) 22

C
Canada 14
China 4, 8, 9, 12, 15, 33
chlorofluorocarbons 31
coral bleaching 28, 29

D
dama gazelle 17
Dobson, G. M. B. 31

E
Earth Day 34
elephants 19
Equator 10, 30

F
Fabry, Charles 30

G
giant panda 33
global warming 20, 21,
 24, 25, 27, 28
goitered gazelle 17
Great Plains 17
great white shark 15
Greenland 40

H
halons 31, 44
Hubbert, M. King 32
Hubbert peak 32

I
India 9, 19, 23, 24,
 28, 37, 41

L
League Against
 Cruel Sports 18

M
mammoths 16, 17
Monaco 40
Mongolia 17

N
non-
 renewable 6, 7
North America
 9, 17

O
over-grazing 12
overfishing 14

P
plutonium 36
polyethylene-lined 35

R
radioactive 36
recycle 34, 35, 42, 44
renewable 6, 7
rubbish 5, 34, 35, 42

S
scimitar-horned
 oryx 17
shahtoosh 19
shark fin soup 15
stratosphere 24, 31
styrofoam 35, 44
sulphur dioxide 38

T
Terra
 spacecraft
 25
tigers 19, 32,
 41

toxic waste 36, 37
Tropic of Cancer 10
Tropic of Capricorn 10

U
United States of
 America 9
uranium 36

W
water table 23
whale oil 14
whale shark 15
whaling 14